And

David Flynn

A poem that covers everything.
Here it is:

Now,
let's analyze what we have.
In that white space are atoms.
If we understood just one atom
in every aspect,
every,
we would understand the universe.
Not even one whole atom.
A bit of that atom,
A muon say.
Why does it exist?
What is its purpose?
What is its relationship to God?
Is there a God that relates to the muon?
What happens to the muon after death?
There are an infinite number of questions about the muon,
because we don't know much.
Then there are the quarks,
and the antineutrinos,
and all the detail of physics,
and all that physics and mathematics think are unknowable,
and.

So that will be the title of this poem:
And.
We don't know much,
and what we do know,
the origin of a dust particle say,

is questionable and limited.
There is always an 'and' to every statement we make.

I am going to the grocery store.
And.
I have a headache.
And.
I want to see a movie about murder.
And.
Quantum entanglement.
And.
Consciousness.
And.

Now 'and' questions:
How do I walk across the room?
What do I have for lunch?
Will it rain this afternoon?

Questions, and if there are answers,
and there might not be or it might not be an answer but a possibil-
ity,
then the next statement starts with,
you guessed it,
And.

And.

This poem is endless, actually.
No end to the detail,
no end to the changes,
no end to the mistakes

and corrections
and mistakes in the corrections.

Cats.
We have three.
They see what we don't, ultraviolet.
They smell what we don't.
Their whiskers sense what we don't.
They still like to play with mice,
batting the little creatures around with their paws,
biting the necks,
ripping open the entrails.
They still lick each other's buttholes.
They will sleep twenty hours a day.
What do they dream?
Because they twitch,
their legs moving like they are running.
If a cat were to take a human IQ test he would do poorly:
What number comes next in this series, 34, 15, 68, 30, 22?
Huh?
But if a human was to take a cat IQ test he would do poorly too.
I can't even make up a cat IQ question. I'm that cat stupid.
What comes next for our cats, duck pate, tuna morsels, belly
rub?
I don't know.

So it is with germs, deer, buzzards, trees, grass, everything.
We really have no idea what goes on inside them.
They don't communicate
like we want them to communicate.

Physicists, those crazy theorists, have thought experiments
that state there are multiple bubbles after the Big Bang,

multiple universes.
That because there are so many, an infinity,
there are an infinity of actions.
Say I flip a coin.
In some universes it will be tails.
In other universes it will be heads.
In other universes it will land on its side.
In other universes it will roll off the table
that way.
In other universes it will roll off the table
that other way.
I live in other universes, but
in some I have blond hair,
in some I have red hair,
in some I am bald.
in some I don't have a head,
in some I have a computer screen on my forehead.
Infinite possibilities.

So And.
Whatever I write today,
tomorrow will be another universe.
I am not working toward a conclusion.
I am working.
And.

And.

Marshmallows.
Or is it marshmellows.
On the end of a stick,
held in the flames of a fire,
the gooey white and the black seer

taste good.
Good.
Meaning
sugary burnt and, yes, gooey.
And
what is there about a fire,
the wood piled,
outdoors,
preferably not in a backyard
but in the forest,
that leads to ghost stories,
sing-a-longs
and sighs.

And
World War Two.
My father didn't fight in World War Two,
although he served in it.
Seabees.
Naval engineering corps.
Helped build an air strip in Okinawa.
And is his picture of women near a door
a brothel?
Don't know.
Never will know.
I have a chest made out of downed Japanese plane parts,
metal strips and such.
Seabee insignia spray painted on the top.
Yeh, a bee.
Vietnam, Iraq, my lifetime.
Not the same.
World
war.

And a righteous one at that.
Nazis.
Hitler ranting.
Japanese nationalists.
The Emperor is divine.
Seems weird
that millions on millions of people,
Germans, Japanese,
would give their lives, their living
on proving their superiority
through fireballs.
But that's humans.
Germans now seem nice;
Japanese too.
I had an elderly Japanese man
at a party in Osaka
come up to me, push his finger toward my face, and say,
"Maybe I killed your father."
"No. My father lived for many decades after the war."
"Then maybe I killed your father's friends."
Maybe. Could Be.
I can't say the Japanese man and I became pals,
but we came to a kind of agreement.
Americans killed Japanese; Japanese killed Americans.
Might happen again.
Governments're crazy.
Populations follow governments.
See you in the fireball.
Hiroshima.
Pearl Harbor.
Been there.
Love, charity, care.
Only in the intervals.

As I learned in war zones, Macedonia, Israel,
morals and beliefs are sweet,
but in time of war screw those.
Survival is all that counts.

Somehow I have managed to live to 72 and haven't killed any-
body.
Dodged the Vietnam draft.
Damm Republican war.
Got old.
I think not killing someone I didn't know is an achievement.
Give me that trophy, that certificate.
At least applaud.

Yet it is true that without our Army, Navy, Air Force, Marines,
etc.
we would be slaves, or dead, or meat.
Because of the other Armies, Navies, Air Forces, Marines.
Nuclear bombs.
The illusion that the individual, me, you, is important.
Nobody pushes me around.
Every cell in your body is pushed around daily by businesses,
governments, philosophers, priests.
And.

O.K.
I'll never finish this thought, except with a Five-Paragraph
Outline type conclusion,
which is artificial.
I am not writing the artificial.
So The End
For today.
Just because I have stuff to do.

And.
And.
And.

And.
Sore knees.
Foggy head.
No goal.
Yeah, that's today.
But.
And.
There's always the next.
Better.
Worst.
The same.
Then death.

Yeah, I know.
Cliché-ville.
You live, you struggle, then you die.
You hurt, you medicate, you swing your fists, then you die.
Your voice soars, you become a billionaire, you invent great
devices, then you die.
Old story. Everybody knows it. Nobody can change it. We are
doomed. Boo hoo. Snippets.
Ordinary day.

I don't know what to tell you.
Continue. We don't have a choice.
Don't expect conclusions, for
if there is a conclusion
it's just part of a longer thing.

I love "thing".
Could be any "thing".
You win the lottery.
Now what?
Can't buy love.
Sure you can.
Can buy sleep.
Can buy the car you want.
Can buy a trip around the world.
But who wins the lottery?
Not me. Not even close.
The odds of winning the lottery are fantastically less than the
odds of being killed in a car crash
on the way to buying the ticket.
Conclusion 1. Conclusion 2. Conclusion 3.
Each of our lives has billions of conclusions.
Then you die.

Walking without certainty.
Smiling without triumph.
Thinking without a destination.

Then you die.

And.

And.
Chance.
Good name for a horse.
Good first name for a baby.
Chance's shoes.
Chance's haircut.

Chance's dissertation.
Chance.
It's all chance,
So that's important.
You see a job ad on the computer,
you apply.
Someone at the company reads yours among the thousands
and happens to choose it.
You get the job.
You move to Dayton, Ohio.
There you meet your future wife at a friend's backyard barbe-
cue.
That night in November
you have sex.
The sperm, one of millions, attaches to that egg, one of a lot.
And there she is,
your daughter,
Meghan Valerie.
So your boss happens to be a soccer fan.
Not many soccer fans in Dayton, Ohio, at the time.
You are too.
What are the odds.
He likes you.
You two go to a middle school soccer game.
He gives you a promotion.
A five-bedroom house happens to be on sale then,
the owner fired from his job and going bankrupt.
You buy it at a good price.
So brick house in a snotty neighborhood,
promotion at work,
wife,
daughter.

Everything else.
Chance.

We believe that we think our way to decisions.
We are wrong.
Belief is another chance.
I think I am for this political party.
My father was in that party.
Chance.

And.
Cheese.
The wedge happened to be at the grocery store.
I happened to look at it in the cooler.
Some connection previously made in my brain:
cheese good.
I buy it.

And.

And.
So forth.
Go forth.
A new day.
What will I do with it?
Live.
Sleep.
It's a day not an era.
I don't believe in eras anyway.
The planet is a lot messier than that.
It's midnight, so now everybody on Earth will start believing in
Realism.

It's midnight, so now everybody on Earth will live in the Com-
puter Age.
We human are messy.
Face it.
Attempts by logic, by belief(s), by authoritarianism can't file the
world.
We are not straight lines.
We aren't lines at all.
The way we think is only one of many systems that make a
person,
and the way we think is actually the many ways we think.
Messy.
A perfectly logical person would be a horror.

So a new day.
Just like the other days.
Sun rises above the horizon;
the dark becomes light;
I can see,
though the cats saw way before me, the black.
Sun rises above me; sun lowers below me.
Twilight.
Night.
You know the plot.
Day the sun explodes,
no day.
Day the Earth wobbles;
different day.
Day the Gamma Storm floods the planet,
we're dead.
Days.
They are boring,
But they are all we have,

except for nights.
One sense, sight, less.

And.
tangles.
Much more representative of life than, say, sticks.
Even tangles isn't right.
Too clear.
Hairs can be separated, seen each, untangled.
I am just trying to deal with immense complexity.

Doomed.
Well, we all are.
So what does that require of us?
That we focus on what we have?
Yeah, but don't think that makes us profound.
Does my thought on how to make the best scrambled eggs live after my body dies?
Doubt it.
Doomed.
So, sure, I am going to enjoy my lunch.
Might add some cantaloupe chunks to the plate.
Focus on what we have.
But be a priest too.
Consider eternity.
Consider it.
Don't eat it.

And.

And.
War.

I dodged the draft during the Vietnam War by going to college.
Glad I did.
It wasn't patriotism to kill a lot of Vietnamese because,
well, I still don't understand why.
I admire those who did go,
some dying,
including a friend of mine from high school.
Another friend still has psychological problems
because he was at the massacre at Mai Lai.
And what.
Communism versus capitalism.
Shows the individual human is nothing.
The power,
the government,
the structure
is the big deal.

For fifty years I have lived between huge wars,
although there have been disasters like Iraq.
More dumb government.
I also realize this is a period that is unusual.
Some people in the past lived in war their whole lives.
Bombs or their threat every day. Bullets.
Hasn't made my life any easier,
just more individual.

I lived a few months each in two war-like zones.
Israel in 1993 during the first Intifada.
Almost died by a nail bomb in the Beersheba bus station, sitting
next to a box.
PLO operatives invaded the town where I lived, Mizpe Ramon,
And shot up the restaurant where I would be most days for
lunch.

Macedonia in 2001.
The incursion from Kosovo managed to cover half of the 12
miles from the border to Skopje
where I lived.
From then on no car lights at night.
My favorite ice cream parlor near my apartment was blown up,
Albanski owned, Slavic bomb.
Three on the embassy scale one day.
Everybody else in the program left; I stayed.
The students were surprised to see me walk into the classroom.
One day we tried to discuss *The Great Gatsby*, but helicopter
gunships roared overhead
 again and again.
"So why are we reading about these silly rich drunks from the
American 1920s when we could die
at any moment?" I, the teacher, asked.
The conclusion was that during wartime, survival was all,
but the students were learning more about what to do during
normal times,
which they all were aiming for.
I left on an airplane which could be destroyed by rebel rockets at
any second.
When ten minutes, exactly, had passed one passenger started
clapping.
The whole airplane clapped and relief filled the seats.
We were out of rocket range.

Today is pretty peaceful,
A few war spots in Africa, the Middle East,
but not where I live.
I can wake up, drink my coffee, read my magazines,
and sit at this computer writing poetry.
I might die on the interstate in my car,

or in the hospital with the virus,
or from a gang member with a pistol.
I'll die somehow.
But not in a mass attack,
a nuclear bomb,
a drone,
swarms,
warfare.

Is human history the history of wars,
or the history of thought?
Wars.

And.

And.
Food.
One of life's joys,
The taste,
the look,
the smell,
the texture on our tongues.
A casserole say.
Bubbly cheese,
yellowy and orangey with islands of steam.
And below,
strings of once-living chicken,
stalks of broccoli trees,
peas like green periods,
rosemary maybe,
cumin maybe.

If we all had to hunt and grow our food it wouldn't be as good.
Our food might hunt us too,
docile cows become wild-eyed killers
or bulls doing their male thing.
Pigs tearing us apart while grunting.
Eagle beaks in our backs.
Some days we might not find food,
so we eat each other.
Cannibalism.
After all, we are meat.
The eyes might be good in a soup.
Brain like meat cauliflower.
Penis.
Breasts.
Heart.
I ate raw horse heart in a restaurant in Japan one time, so why
not raw human heart.
Liver, fried.
Glands, maybe. Who knows?

For today though the grocery store chain had 1,000s of square
feet of food
others had grown and harvested and slaughtered.
Packaged.
At check out I put the food on the belt,
a rectangle of misery.
Chicken fingers?
Dead clucking chickens loving life and fighting weakly to live.
Cows drilled to death in the forehead.
Living spinach plants reaching for the sun, then cut off at the
stalk.
For dinner I will eat tragedies.

Such is life.
We live off the life force of others,
though we call it protein or carbohydrates or some such.
No wonder vampires are so popular in books and movies.
We are all vampires,
just not dead or sleeping in coffins.

So yes, I have to quit this and eat lunch.
I will,
of course,
enjoy the taste.
What lives went into my jar of pimento cheese
with jalapenos.
I don't want to think about it.
Just eat, enjoy and live another day.
Thanks, dead things.
Got to feed those gut microbes too.
Everything in the universe is a killer.
Neutrino killing atom.
Can't let my conscience starve me to death.

Lunch.

And.

And.
I once wrote a poem titled "Better Asleep Than Awake",
and today is one of those days.
I didn't want to wake up,
didn't want to get out of bed,
didn't want my life.
I am not suicidal.
Don't mistake despair for destruction.

I just don't want to do what I will be doing until more sleep
tonight.

If I could just fly somewhere new,
somewhere I have never been.
Argentina, South Africa, Dubai, Perth, Antarctica.
Or somewhere I have been but would like to go again.
Israel, Japan, Indonesia, India, Italy, Ireland, Brazil.
But no.
The pandemic has stopped all air travel to so many places,
even New Mexico where I wanted to visit this summer.
Alone with myself,
I want other company.

Facing though,
today will be inside this condo.
These walls,
that same food in the refrigerator,
cable surfing,
worrying.
My wife works from home.
On her office door is a sign that reads:
"Zoom Session".
Means stay away;
stay quiet.

So here I am
with the infinite pages in Word.

And.

Ice cream sandwiches.
The idea is to focus on small pleasure.

We don't understand ice cream sandwiches
the same way we don't understand the afterlife,
dark matter,
God,
love.
But we do know they taste good,
the chill of vanilla ice cream,
the throb of the chocolate.
Not our usual feelings.
The ice cream sandwich at least tastes, one of the five senses.
Maybe add sight to that, it looks.
We don't understand the ice cream sandwich molecules
or why the ice cream sandwich
or love and the ice cream sandwich
or logical positivism and the ice cream sandwich.
But it tastes cold.
Good enough for today.

I still wish I was asleep.
But I can't
so I won't.

And.

Not a good day of writing poetry,
but it is now over.

And.

I know.
Ice cream sandwiches are so trite, so mundane, so cheezey,
to mix foods.
The horror is I used it, wrote about it, it came to mind.

Won't undo that.
Won't edit it.
There it is.

And.

I wrote something.
Couldn't do that asleep.
Good for me.

And.

And.
Lingering lessons about legality.
Mostly manneristic matinees.
Quirky quintessential quandrums.

Ugh.
I will have to delete those.
Or keep them as samples of how my mind, your mind, our minds
can access the random.
We often don't think about the subject we want only.
It is hard for me to pray, for example.
My mind will wander to this issue, to a person, to sex.
So that if we do get there,
there being the issue brought to a conclusion,
it is often through this and that, here and there, a roomful of
mazes.
And by conclusion I mean,
not the end,
not the answer,
but a point we can stand on.
And take those thoughts through a day,

a week,
a year,
a life,
and our ideas are more a dance called the Herky Jerky
than a marathon run.
We stay in the same place,
though we have moved right angle, right angle, right angle,
straight, circle, right angle.

And.
I wrote a lot of poetry in my near sleep last night,
not sleeping but alliterating.
It was good.
This morning,
It isn't good.
Alliteration connects,
like rhyme.
Survival, revival; naval, upheaval. Rhyme. Off rhyme.
Love, lechery, licentiousness, lust. Alliteration.
Were those connections in my brain,
or connections in the sound only?
Worms, waste, wanton, won ton, wagging, warm, wanna be,
witch hunt, wig wam, Waxahatchie,
womanly, wam bam thank you m'am, worse, worst, wurst,
wander, like here, womb, we.
Worms.
Back to death.

So look at those words and see what my mind is like this morn-
ing?
Not really.
But all minds contain all things we have encountered.
Memory.

And from those we take what is happening before our five
senses,
now,
this nano-slice,
and combine them with a chunk of what we have stored.
Like
this coffee cup in front of me.
Brown earth
because of the stain.
Native American petroglyphs
because of marks in the stain.
I had to look up petroglyph, "Native American drawings in
rocks."
And from that combination
not much of importance
today.
Clean the coffee cup,
maybe.

And.

I really, truly, strongly need to leave this condo.
Quarantine is important, and I am doing it.
Still, I have to fight this wind inside me.
Rain this afternoon,
and I am trapped again.
I don't want to be stuck with myself.
Got to have new input.
Even if it's the same old grocery store.
The same old interstate.
The same old music in the car.
Gary Moore, the B-52's, The 5, 6, 7, 8's, Steely Dan,
Random sound from long ago on the radio stations.

Did you know that Steely Dan was a metal dildo
in William Burrough's novel *Naked Lunch*?
Yep.
Don't know why the group chose that for a name.
Random access to my brain, like I said.

The 5, 6, 7, 8's are a Japanese hard rock group, cute little girls
that scream and bang.
They're really good.

And.
See you tomorrow.
Have a day that isn't a disaster.

And.
Rambling Man, like the song says.
That's more profound that Systematized Man,
because the system is always wrong.
Sometimes focusing, but
always wrong.

And.

And.
Riboflavin.
That's a blast from my past.
TV commercials bragged that their food product contained
riboflavin.
Amazing what makes up our minds.
I had a dream last night where the main character,
me?,
searched for a box that played music.
Sticks containing the music were placed inside the box,
and the box played the songs.

Monks were standing there, so this had something to do with my
Catholic upbringing.
The box was missing last night,
but lots of the sticks and some sheets that also played music
were found in a room.
Finally, in a different monk's quarters,
the box,
though dirty and unused.
I had that dream maybe 65 years ago.
The box worked well then.
For all those years the dream was stored somewhere in the folds
of my brain.
Last night the dream came out.
Why?
Don't know.
Nothing reminded me of the box,
Although I did check the monastery in Kentucky
where I go on retreats twice a year,
and found it is still closed
because of the pandemic.
That?

Such are our brains.
Every sight, every sound, every thought, every dream, ever is still
in there.
Even if we are senile, they are there, just not accessible as much.
Storage.
That should be all our names.
Hi, Storage. How you doing?
Not bad, Storage. You?

So why aren't I wise?
I don't know anything.

I have less faith in my thoughts day by day.
Including that one.
Storage, yes.
Bringing the bits together, much much less.
So bits, strong.
Overall, not.
Consciousness, weak.
Reason, LOL.
Intuition, gimme a break.
ESP, NOT.
We face the world as a random mosaic of color, not a thing,
things.
We are abstract paintings,
but not even that.
Put the canvas in the back yard,
and let it be rained on, snowed on, bugged on, whatever
for a year,
ten years,
thirty years.
That is us.
Our brains don't come together;
they just contain more bits.

Life is so complicated because
we can't make life One.

And.

And.
I am a big romantic.
That means I walk around in a fog of feeling,
warmth, love, enjoyment, admiration.
Of people, of colors, of birds, of walls, of trees,

most, but not all, of everything and everyone.
I am not an optimist.
I am a middleist.
This happens, that happens, some good, some bad, some medio-
cre.
O.K.
That's what I have.
Better than blind, no legs, and an oxygen tube in my nose.
So far, so life.
Haven't conquered; haven't been defeated totally; haven't ruled;
haven't been ruled
totally.
A romantic.
Not technically.
I don't believe that feelings are the way to know the world.
Feelings are regulated by the brain, which can be mistaken.
I can feel joy at seeing someone,
then that someone betray me.
I can feel happiness at watching my team on TV,
then that team lose,
and others watch their teams with happiness on TV,
then those teams lose.
Or win, and it's the next day, and the bills come, and my knees
hurt, and I am alone, and crap.
Logic, no.
Logically we have killed millions not of our kind.
Logically we have developed multiple theories of the same thing,
like the purpose of life,
God, god,
or the behavior of a candle flame.
Intuition.
No.
Different intuitions inside different people lead to different actions,

like crystal balls, accurate or just rock.
I am a romantic because my feelings are strong,
not because I think those feelings are precise.
The opposite.
I walk around in a fog of inaccuracy.
I look at my wife.
Beautiful.
She's stayed.
I believe in her.
A fog of love.
Love is a fog.
Sometimes love can been wrong;
the wrong person,
the abuser,
the player,
the line speaker.
There are web sites now for those.
But looking at my wife,
at her desk working from home,
a medical record on the monitor,
a case to mediate,
I am in a romantic fog of feeling.
And if then,
why not any time?
Red hair to her waist.
Cabernet lips.

A fog, a cloud, a vagueness,
that's me.
I approve this message,
as politicians say in their vicious ads.
Because this is a good way to live through a day.
Better than nettles or ghost chili peppers.

It's not that I'm a fool,
at least not a big fool.
I see car crashes, pandemic, hatreds and class structure.
It's just that
I see cardinals, rainbows (Yes, I know how sappy that is), and I
see really old people holding hands.
They mean nothing,
but
if I am looking for a whole, an entireity, everything,
they are there with the pain too.
A chili bowl full of . . .
Even the dumbest of metaphors.

So today I am not right either.
I just am alive.
Good enough for this Thursday.
Won't go to Mars, the first human.
Won't cure the virus.
Won't write the right thought about why.
Just,
yet again,
alive.

And.

And.

Formaldehyde.
No telling what pops up in my mind.
Rebus.
Dewey decimal system.
But those go nowhere.
Instead, let's try love.

Love makes the world go round.
No, it doesn't; that's gravity or some such.
I will love you forever.
Or until I or you die.
Are there married couples in heaven?
What happens if somebody has been married more than once?
I knew somebody who was working on her fifth marriage.
Love.
With 7 billion humans currently on Earth there has to be a way to
make them work together.
Tribes.
That's one basic human trait.
To divide into groups, us versus them.
The group may be small as a nuclear family.
It can be large as a race.
We are all part of many tribes,
nuclear family like I said,
political party,
religion—and last I heard there were more than 20,000 official
divisions of Christianity,
First Church of the Redeemer, Second Church of the Redeemer,
Third Church of the Redeemer.
A church near my city divided in two over the issue of should
there be applause after baptism.
Now one half thinks the other half will burn in hell forever
because they do or do not allow applause
after baptism.
Tribes.
Sports team fans.
White collar, blue collar.
College graduate, high school non-graduate.
Humanities, STEM.
Tribes.

Today I am in the I-like-salmon tribe.
Many are in the I-don't-like-salmon tribe.
And other tribes also, too numerous to think about.
More brain divisions.

Love bridges tribes,
bridges so many things.
That's why it is so important.
Without love we would be constantly at war.
Without love there would be no families,
no children. Well maybe.
Too much hatred in politics,
particularly in the Trump administration.
Followers slobber hatred of Hispanics, of Chinese, of those they
disagree with.
A nation of tribes
And not of love.

I love you.

And.

And.
Little sleep last night.
Worries.
Tossing from side to side
literally.
And now
the Holy Roman Empire.
No idea why that popped into my mind.
It was neither Holy nor Roman nor an Empire.
Read that somewhere.
Democracy is in trouble,

even in America.
Maybe I am worried about that.
It's either taking advantage of the thoughts and talents of hun-
dreds of millions of people
or
the thoughts and talents of say 1000,
while the rest of us do the physical work.
Money rules America now.
Takes millions just to run for mayor.
I fear for the next twenty years.
America was such an experiment,
imperfect,
always poor versus rich,
but with some attention made to the bottom 90 percent.
Now
tyranny looms.
Land of the Free, Freedom of Religion, the Statue of Liberty
welcoming immigrants.
 I am saddened that Their use of hatreds has gotten results.

I had a landlord in Boston whose name was Green.
One day he told me why.
His grandfather or great-grandfather, I forgot,
arrived from Poland and was processed on Ellis Island.
He had a long long Polish name.
The man behind the desk was tired.
The ancestor was to be his last immigrant of the day.
He just couldn't deal with the long name.
The ancestor wore a green coat.
So, family name Green.
And now generations later it was still Green.
Talk about naturalization.

A new month today.
I dread the squares on the calendar,
31 of them.

I need a nap.
Awake, you have more hours today than I have.
I hope they are not stormy.
Of course it would be fabulous if they were victorious, joyful,
loving.
We'll see after I wake up.

And.

I don't feel like I should stop here for the day.
Not satisfied.
So.
I belong to God.
Don't know what God is.
Don't know what belong might be.
Not sure there will be an I after my death.
But
I belong to God.
Whatever.

That's my prayer for today.

My prayer for tomorrow might be I wish this damn virus would
go away.
Of course it won't.
We face another year of masks and quarantine and deaths.
The Plague Year II, or is it III, or IV?
The mighty virus, too small for humans to see,
has won for the moment.

That should make us humble,
but doesn't.
Pandemics in the future, V, VI, VII, VIII.
Climate change.
Unusable portions of the Earth for humans.
Miami under water.
No polar bears.
World War III?
Nothing I can do except die.
I need a nap.
Wake up thinking about the good things,
Love,
food,
poems,
trees,
wild turkeys,
song.
And not
flies,
ants,
coughs,
pain,
hobbling.

Good night,
even though it's not even noon yet.
I am going to take a nap.
Dream about a blue tomorrow.
Enjoy my delusion
for a couple of hours.

And.

I have been thinking the last few days about three of my oldest friends who died.
I am 72.
It is inevitable that everyone will die eventually.
Child actors.
Rock stars.
Boxers.
Everyone.
But these three did not live the average male age, now 78.
My family is gone too,
mother, father, grandfathers, grandmothers, great-aunt, great-uncle.
I have two cousins, but they don't communicate.
So basically with my best friends gone too I am floating in space, nobody in view.

Joe Simmler.
Joe was my college roommate at the University of Missouri.
We shared a house together my senior year.
I was an usher in his wedding.
He met his future bride at the Missouri library.
He came back to the house one night.
And said,
I was sitting on the other side of a study table,
one of those with a barrier in the middle,
when the most beautiful woman I have ever seen smiled at me,
and sat on the other side.
I couldn't study.
I couldn't think.
I had my notebook out and for the first time in my life I wrote a poem,
to her.
I ripped it from the notebook, signed it "Joe", folded it, and

pushed it over the top.
As soon as I did I panicked.
What if she screamed.
What if she called security.
There was a long, long pause
then she looked around the side.
'I like your poem,' she said.
I asked her to the Heidelberg
for a beer.
She said yes.

Joe and I kept contact all the years after.
I visited him in Seattle twice, once in the 1970s when, unem-
ployed,
I drove around the U.S. trying to get a newspaper job.
They lived in a suburb, and had a big dog.
I visited him again 40 years later.
My wife had a business trip to Seattle and I went along.
Joe met us for dinner at a seafood restaurant.
The view was the sweep of Seattle's waterfront.
Then a couple of years later I got a call from his wife.
She was gasping.
Joe had died.
A sudden attack.
But he had seemed so healthy.
And there one of my oldest friends was gone.
I couldn't react to absence.
A hole.
A zone of nothing.

Johnny Windrow.
Windrow put a shotgun to his heart and pulled the trigger.
The family asked that I tell people he died of heart problems.

I had known him more than 50 years.
His family's house was out Windrow Road from Brownsville, TN.
We went to the University of Missouri together,
fellow journalism students.
One day Johnny said he wanted me to meet somebody near
Brownsville,
and that somebody was Sleepy John Estes,
the blues singer.
"Drop Down Momma."
We went to his shotgun house,
which was later moved to a park near the interstate.
I visited Windrow in San Diego on my drive around the country
looking for work, stayed with him and his first wife.
He was in the Navy, a boiler room mechanic on a warship.
His second wife was the daughter of a former vice president of
the Philippines, Pat.
Minneapolis, Honolulu, Johnny moved around, working for
newspapers.
He wrote novels too, set in West Tennessee.
In one of them was a lawyer named Flynn.
Yeah, he confirmed that was me.
Part of the year he lived in the Philippines at Pat's family com-
pound,
and part of the year the couple lived in a condo in Brownsville.
So we talked on a Thursday.
He had been nominated for Best Humorous Column,
one he wrote for the Brownsville newspaper,
and we were going to the Tennessee Press Association awards
dinner
together.
That Monday I got an email from the newspaper's editor.
Johnny had put a shotgun to his chest, his heart, and pulled the
trigger.

At the funeral everybody was surprised as I was,
although everybody also mentioned the drinking.
Apparently he had had a DUI wreck the week before.
Maybe that.
Who knows?
There was no note from this writer.
At the gravesite I talked to Pat.
Some didn't because they resented her not being with Johnny,
 even blamed her for his death.
She had flown from the Philippines and was tired.
She hadn't wanted to live in Brownsville.
Too many looked down on her as not-white.
She was numb, no idea why her husband had killed himself.
He had talked about living with her full-time in the Philippines.
But pull the trigger,
explode the heart,
and he was gone.
Johnny's two sisters stood by the grave.
I had known them since they were little girls.
One had become the "lesbian troubadour."
One had married a waiter from Italy.
Just before the casket was lowered into the hole in the ground
the funeral company employee opened a large box.
White doves flew out and then over the adjoining field.
Still talking to Pat and the sisters I stayed awhile after the others
left.
The doves flew back,
trained,
for food,
professionals.
A long-time friend was dead.
Another one.
Another one I had assumed would always be there.

The Catholic church taught that all suicides go to hell.
They had despaired of God's love.
I can't think that of Johnny Windrow.
He was a good man,
A life-long friend.

And.

Phillip Scott.
Phillip was my oldest real friend.
I met him the first day of high school.
He lived out in the country, and not Bemis, TN,
my home town.
For the next almost 60 years we were close friends,
even though he stayed in the country
on his mother's property,
and I roamed the world,
Hawaii, Japan, you name it.
Phillip could be cutting,
often,
but somehow we kept going.
He wrote a series of murder mysteries set around my home
town,
cast metal military figures.
I visited his house on that country road
every time I happened to be back.
And I did return, like Bemis was my center post,
and I was on a string,
buzzing in a circle.
We went to a University of Tennessee football game together
a year before his death,
a long drive, hundreds of miles East.
Pancreatic cancer.

He wanted us to visit Shiloh Military Park,
as we often had,
one last time before he died,
but by then he was too weak to leave the house.
A hospital bed in the living room.
He underwent chemotherapy,
but it was so horrible,
he decided to quit,
and to die.
At least he had a few weeks when he knew he was going to be dead.
As opposed to being hit by a tractor trailer rig on the interstate,
or having that sudden heart attack in your sleep.
I was asked to give a speech at the memorial at the funeral home
he had instead of a standard funeral.
What could I say?
How many adventures did we have over 60 years?
We went to the Beatles together,
the Rolling Stones.
We saw a baseball game in Kansas City with Mike Walls,
a friend also dead.
So many nights:
car chases,
fights,
basketball games.
So I spoke about our friendship.
If ever there were friends it was him and me.
The day we sneaked into a movie my parents forbade me to see,
James Bond.
Oh a thousand times.
Phillip is dead.
They all die.
I die.
You die.

And there are others I have known too, dead and living.
Through Facebook I have made connections with many,
right wing fanatics especially.
Threads anyway.

So it is with everybody.
Everybody you know will die.
Everybody you've ever heard of will die.
Forgotten?
Maybe not soon after,
but a hundred years from then.
Two hundred years from then.
We all change the world just by walking down the street.
That's our legacy.
I once wrote: "As if we had walked through a field / and that
field a year later."
I want that on my tombstone, memorial stone, whatever.
Along with
"Where before he was at one point / now he is everywhere."
I wrote those lines about Dan Schroeder,
a friend who died in a motorcycle accident
when I was in my 20s.

Three good friends dead.
Four.
And I'm 'just' 72.
The past is in my brain,
and that brain is doomed.
Sounds sad, doesn't it?
It really isn't.
Everybody on Earth,
all 7 billion now,

is the same way.
Die naturally.
Death is an adventure
if we remain conscious.

I don't want to write about death anymore.
Think the next thing will be dancing.
I inhabit the groove.

And.

I have decided to keep writing this poem until work starts a week
from next Monday.
Then it will be all work.
Until then
I can wander,
I can connect thought with thought,
I can check to see what I am thinking about
sub-consciously
or maybe consciously but without words.
So today I am thinking about

frogs.
Frogs don't say 'rivet.'
Once I had a residency at the Millay Colony in Massachusetts,
the Berkshires.
Out a dirt road.
Every day I took a walk up a long dirt path to the tennis court
where Edith St. Vincent Millay used to play.
Spooky.
All that was left was the grass court, and the posts on the side
where the net should have been.
Nobody played.

Except ghosts maybe.
At the bottom of the hill was a pond covered with green scum
and lily pads.
Every time I passed the pond a roar of frogs erupted,
one huge noise, ugly and frog-like.
I mentioned this to one of the other writers in residency,
and he said,
They are challenging you, a stranger.
If you know the right noise to make, the right message,
they will stop and let you join them in the pond.
So, sure, I tried.
A few times as I passed the pond and the noise began
I tried to imitate what I heard.
Not rivet but brach brach.
The pond just grew louder,
more challenge.
But one magical day I tried again,
Brach brach,
And the pond instantly became silent.
Like a switch had been pulled to off.
I could have joined my fellow frogs in the pond,
maybe on a lily pad,
although I actually didn't see any frogs that day.
Instead I just laughed
and walked on up the hill to the tennis court.
For a few seconds though,
I was a frog,
welcomed by my friends the frogs.
All it took was the right 'words'.
I have no idea why that day's response worked
and the other day's didn't.
but it did.

So what is the worst thing I have ever eaten in my life?
I was in Taipei, Taiwan, at a restaurant in the hotel where I was
staying.
The menu was all in Chinese characters, which I couldn't read,
except for one item, in English,
"Frog Spit."
The waiter was no help;
he couldn't speak any English.
So I did what I had done before when I couldn't read the menu,
pick a couple of items at random.
To that I added, of course, Frog Spit.
Later I learned that 'frog spit' is Asian slang for
pond scum.
It means something else in England,
the white bubbles where frogs lay their eggs
for protection and nourishment.
But there in Taiwan it meant pond scum.
And when the bowl arrived
it indeed
looked like pond scum.
Green.
Slimy.
I of course not only had to sample it, but use my spoon to sip a
pretty good amount
to save face with the waiter.
Did he and the cook have a good laugh back in the kitchen?
I don't know, but he stood looking at me.
I also don't know if the bowl was literally full of pond scum,
or if the 'soup' just looked like pond scum.
It tasted like pond scum,
yukky and coating my tongue.
Back in my room I drank a few glasses of water,
but

didn't help.
The worst thing I have ever eaten.
Frog Spit.

And.

So today, frogs.
They are what came to mind.

Oh
And eating frog legs at the Catfish Hotel.
When I was a kid my family drove to Shiloh,
about 60 miles from our house,
to the Catfish Hotel
on the Tennessee River.
I loved the frog legs.
They tasted like nothing else I had ever eaten
and not the chicken everybody said they did.
Then the paper plant up river
was fined for dumping mercury in the water.
The next time I had frog legs at the Catfish Hotel,
yep,
they tasted like chicken.

I don't believe in necessity,
obviously,
nor much in system,
except as a way we humans cope,
and not as a way to truth.
It is entirely arbitrary to say I am going to keep writing this poem
until a week from Monday,
but it would be entirely arbitrary if I said I am going to write a
14-line sonnet,

or a 39-line sestina,
or an epic with its requirements,
or iambic pentameter.
The day after I stop, the poem goes on.
I just won't be writing it,
and you, reader, won't be reading it.

Then on to whatever happens next.

And.

A terrible day.
I would like to pack up, jump in my car, and head out on the
interstate.
I can see myself coming to the intersection.
Left or Right?
West or East?
Of course, it wouldn't save me.
My brain follows me where ever I go.
Might escape a problem or two,
but many would remain.
New ones would rise.
I am my brain.

So let's see what my brain comes up with today.
Cemeteries.
Figures.

My family is buried in Calvary Cemetery, Jackson, TN.
Mother father grandfather grandmother buried side by side by
side by side
beneath a magnolia tree.
Across the cemetery is my great-aunt, great-uncle, other great-

aunts, related husbands and such.
Not for me.

About two miles hike out in the country from my childhood house
of Bemis, TN, is
a Civil War era cemetery.
On top of the graves are items from the dead's life:
tools for a carpenter, toys for a child.
Amazingly in the hundred years between burial and when I last
hiked to see them,
nobody had touched that stuff.

Rumor was a group from my high school including football
players
decided to camp in the Civil War cemetery,
tents, sleeping bags.
Deep into the black night they began to hear noises,
screams, screeches, roars.
They ran.
Had to go back in the daylight to get their gear.
Football players included.
It was disrespectful to camp in a cemetery.
Taught them a lesson.

I, right now, want to be cremated,
but then what?
Kintsugi, a Japanese urn.
Take a beautiful, hand-made urn and throw it on the floor.
Break it into pieces.
Put it back together again with gold.
Sure
but where would the urn be.
Nobody in my life wants my ashes.

Strew the ashes into the river so they float to the sea.
Strew the ashes, me, in places that mean something to me:
my home town, my city, Taos, NM, Japan, Indonesia. Memphis,
the Abbey of Gethsemani.
Lots of paperwork for Japan and Indonesia.
Or maybe, my idea, put them in a metal box, bury them in a
cemetery
or other public place,
and mount a headstone with my name, birth and death years, and
two lines from my poems:
"Where before he was at one place
now he is everywhere."
"As if I had walked through a field
and that field a year later."
As close to immortality and forever as I will get after death
On Earth anyway.
Maybe anywhere.

Would I put the word "Writer" below my name on the head-
stone?
Maybe.
Have to push having been a writer,
especially after I am gone.

I once had a college roommate who was really bad at writing.
He was making a D in his freshman composition class.
He paid me to write an essay for him.
I did.
He was from New York, and I had never been anywhere near
there then.
But I wrote a simple essay about how the city, the noise, the
people
drove him crazy so he would walk to his favorite cemetery.

There in the quiet, among the dead, he felt more at ease.
His mind cleared.
He got an A.

So, am I death-haunted, morbid, sick of life?
Not really,
More than average.
Today is a terrible day.
Terrible connects with death, maybe.
Fangs dripping with blood.
Ghosts who want us dead.
The living dead, humans walking stiffly looking for brains to eat.
I am just a human.
Will rise to the occasion.
Will make it through this one day.
A week, probably,
A Month, probably.
A Year, likely.
Five years, maybe.
Ten years, less maybe.
Twenty years, 50/50.
Let's bet.
I say I live ten more years, but not twenty.
Place your bet.
The insurance company bets that I won't live a lot longer.
Now it's your turn.

And.

And.

Off day.
Handyman fixing the doors.

Bang noise.
I can only write about noise
when there is noise.

Silence.
Many people are afraid of silence.
Like the tomb.
Except our hearing will be gone anyway.
Alone with ourselves.
Except we always are.
Alone with ourselves.

Dogs barking next door.
No idea, no realization, no inspiration.
To think we need no distractions,
so we are all brain.

I think I won't write much today.
Bang bang bang.
Fixing the closet door.
I need the closet door.
And there goes the sonnet,
the prose poem,
the communication.
Door for poem.
Today it's the door.

And.

Hippopotamus.
Spadassinicide.
Hemidemisemiquaver.

Like good food is to taste,
good sounds are to hearing.
Good sights,
a mountain vista,
her face,
a sunset red purple and orange
are to sight
like
of silk,
of skin,
of a breeze
are to touch.
The smell of bacon frying in a pan,
the smell of her,
the smell of him,
the smell of lavender.

We are our senses.
Without them we would be metal boxes.
We take what the senses give us,
and our brain stores, manipulates and orders that.
Locked in:
people who cannot communicate,
but maybe they still sense,
a touch on the arm,
the smell of disinfectant,
the noise of a vacuum cleaner,
the eyes open, but not reporting in words
seeing nurses, the doctor, the ceiling.
The taste of the nutrient.

I haven't grown tired of any sense;
glad I have them all,

Wish I had more.
Dogs, I have read, see in ultraviolet.
Cats see in the dark.
Trees talk in chemicals
we don't hear.
Hippos communicate with dung.
And what else is out there we don't sense.
Dark matter and energy, 95 percent of all creation,
we can't even detect with billion dollar colliders.
We have to give in; we are not wise.
Is an owl really wise?
No, but he knows a few things we don't.
The goal is to live without knowing our purpose, our future, our
world.
To live without truth.
We can think about our fellow humans and how we relate to
them,
but we can't think about the spirit world, if it exists,
and we relate to the dead
without belief,
without communication from God.
To live well: what does that mean?
Another question mark.
We are waist deep in question marks.

Having said that I will enjoy my lunch today,
pimento cheese with jalapenos between whole wheat bread
slices,
a sandwich.
How did we live before the Earl of Sandwich?
Like how did we live thinking the Earth was only 8,000 years old,
or that our island was produced during incestuous sex between a
god and a goddess.

Or that appliances are sacred.
Or that sticking a folded piece of paper in a wall in Jerusalem
sends a message directly to the deity.
I won't worry about those things.
I will enjoy the pimento cheese with jalapeno,
a few chunks of pineapple,
some Scoops,
and a glass of milk
Followed by a chocolate chip cookie.
I will.
That is profound.
Dialectical material is not profound,
unless we follow it.
Food.
So basic
I would get down on all fours and eat grass if I had to.
I would not get down on all fours to read Spinoza.

Anti-intellectual.
Not at all.
I enjoy the thinkers,
as I do a good baseball game.
They are intricate; they are sharp; they are wrong,
but we need them.
We need rules to live by, or else we go in circles.
Maimonides.
Popper.
Derrida.
Wittgenstein.
St. Augustus.
Merton.
Bede.
Barth.

We need to detail the cloud.
Just as
we need poets, short story writers, novelists, essayists
to detail the cloud.
I am proud to be a writer,
a title I have insisted on
though there are few officials who say so.
We are all useless, but essential.
But so is the president,
so is the heart surgeon,
so is the contractor.

I am swatting at balls thrown my way today,
and missing.
Don't see the thrower,
don't have a bat, just my hands,
the balls just white circles.
Ah, I connected, hit one.
My hand hurts,
the ball disappears back into the darkness.

And.

Metaphor.
Can I even think without association.
Truth.
A sword?
A bat?
A chair?
Everything.

And.

Thatching.
When I was in Ireland, early 1990s, I thought about buying a
house on a rural road
of County Monaghan.
The tiny house used to be a post office, but was quaint, beautiful,
Irish.
It was so cheap even I,
a Temporary Assistant Professor at the University of Hawaii,
could afford it,
Less than $10K.
I thought of it as a place to write.
I thought of it as the summers.
Two problems.
It wasn't wired for electricity.
I would have to put a good amount of money into it for the basics.
Why a post office on a one-lane road in rural County Monaghan
had no electricity
I didn't know.
Number two,
it had to be rethatched.
Yes, it was thatched.
Straw?
I knew so little I didn't know what they thatched the roof with.
And that was expensive,
almost as much as the house itself.
And it had to be rethatched every 7 or 8 years.
So I didn't.

Margaret Thatcher.
Make up your own statements.

So now I live in a condo,
a townhouse at the end of a row of townhouses,

in Nashville, Tennessee.
Two stories, not counting the dirt dungeon below.
My office, with peeling paint on the walls,
is upstairs.
Downstairs a high-ceiling living room, a kitchen, two bedrooms,
and a garage filled with boxes and old furniture piled.
And above the garage an unfinished room piled high with plastic
bins, boxes, and things.
A special assessment by the HOA, Homeowners Association, for
a new roof.
We don't need a new roof.
The old one doesn't leak.
But we have to pay for one every few years.
Thatching, shingles, repainting, handyman chores.
We, like everybody, are under attack by insects, heat, rain, dust.
Even our bodies replace the cells, a complete redo every ten
years,
so that we are not the same person as when we were born, and
in fact we have several different bodies during our lifetimes.
Seven in my case.
Brains?
They store the same info, but they too change.
David Flynn 7.
That's me, now.

No wonder we cling to permanence.
That was the Greek urge, unchanging natural laws.
Good if you are a medieval European king, queen, or noble.
Bad if you need change, like a peasant dead at 30, sleeping with
the pigs.
Not good to be creative then.
Not good to want change.
Christianity never changes, they said.

Latin is dead and never changes, so use it.
Not good to rise above you station,
your birth slot in life.
Keep to your assigned place.
The Great Chain of Being.
The king of beasts, #1 for animals.
The king of England, #1 for humans.
#1 for microbes?
Everything in a hierarchy.

Now, hah.
If Apple doesn't come up with a new phone every year we
would think they were in trouble.
Change, new new new new.
Five husbands or five wives in a life.
Can't step twice in the same stream, said another group of
Greeks.
Can't paint the kitchen once in a life; do it over and over again,
new colors, dark light, light dark.
Nothing stays the same. Nothing.

But I like the condo.
Deer graze in the front yard.
Bands of wild turkeys roam our street.
Out the window are trees, leaves, a park.
That all changes of course.
I try to make it the same by saying there are always leaves,
always turkeys, always deer,
but of course,
there will be different leaves next year, bare branches this winter,
turkeys will die and new turkeys will take their place.
Same with deer, even the sweet little fawns.
The same category,

paint,
different actuality,
gray, light blue, cream.

We live in categories
in our minds,
but exist in actualities
in our senses.
Same me,
different body.
My autobiography from birth to death:
the last chapter reads in its entirety, "I died."
But I am not a baby, nor a child, nor a teenager, nor a thirty-year-
old, nor a fifty-year-old.
Now I am seventy-two.
Later, eighty maybe.
Not the same.
I should write a new autobiography every day.

So here I am.
And there you, reader, are.
Let's make the most of here,
But let's not think this is eternity.

And.

The end.
This, of course, isn't really the end of this poem.
It has no end.
I will stop writing, and begin editing in a few days
before I start writing again.
But the poem goes on,
even after I die.

A sonnet, say, has 14 lines,
and is compact as a box.
A small box.
One thought.
One feeling.
But that's impossible.
So a couplet at the end,
to sum up the universe.
I like sonnets a lot.
Sometimes I write them when I haven't written poetry in a while.
They are a good way of getting back on the train.
But they too never end.
The 15th line is always there
on the page,
and the 16th,
etc.

Maybe that should be on my tombstone:
David Flynn, 1948-Death Year.
Etc.

Beyond The End.

My cat Regroup is 17 years old.
That's elderly, really elderly for a cat.
Most cats last about 12 years, I've read.
Regroup is dark, mottled.
She sleeps most of the time
on the carpet or the sofa.
She can still jump down from the sofa,
but needs a lift up.
She is dear to me.

I named her Regroup because of a walk I once took in Hong Kong.
I was on a back street.
All the signs were in Chinese characters except
one:
"Regroup Hair Salon."
I thought that was a great name for a hair salon.
So when I was at the Humane Society,
looking at the cats in cages up for adoption,
I saw this cat.
It looked like my pure-bred Bengal cat Memphis,
who died from an extra tube in his stomach.
He was eating a lot, but it wasn't digested.
Thinner and thinner, bonier and bonier
until I took him to the vet.
The vet operated, trying to remove that tube,
but poor Memphis died on the table.
This cat in the cage looked like Memphis,
but she had just been neutered,
so she was rough looking.
Shaved, tired, irritable.
The sign in Hong Kong popped into my head.
"Regroup!"
"I'll take this one."
17 years later she reaches out a paw and touches my leg,
Snuggles her head into my thigh,
and sleeps.

The End.

And.

An unsettled day.
Dental appointment.

I like to eat, so
I will sit in the chair, mouth open,
While the dentist probes with his metal stick,
looks with his metal mirror.
X-rays maybe.
Without teeth
I would have to 'eat' just Instant Breakfast and soup.
Without food
life is just a series of worries.

I want to write a sonnet.

My dear, why are you so irritable?
Your beautiful face, warm like summer air,
Twists into spit and snarl and mandibles.
I like you better smiling or do not care.

And your hair, dark red, flowing to your waist.
Your hair is the river, the waterfall,
The flood. I have run my fingers through lace
Less soft. Hair that frames your face and calls

Me home from work. Hijab of splendor, life
Itself. The eyes, yes, you have eyes. The lips.
Yes, you have lips. But inside rests my wife,
The beauty, the spirit, the charm. Like whips

Your scowl today bloodies my back, deep pain
Like lightning. So smile. Or at least restrain.

O.K. not great, but I don't want to be consistent.
Prose poetry, sonnet, tanka, ghazal,
paragraphs, anything.

An unsettled day.
May I not crash on the street,
knocking down a light post.

Better later.
Or worse.

And.

Paint.
My office is being repainted.
Plastic sheets cover almost everything except this computer.
A tarp on the floor.
I wonder what this place would be like without paint.
Raw dry wall.
Underflooring
instead of carpeting.
Paint and carpet both cover.
this condo.
Rawness,
but now a smoothness.
It's not just a metaphor to say this condo is like a woman and
make up.
The woman covers up her rawness
with rouge and eyeliner and such.
She's a painting,
some more than others.
This condo is a painting too,
a picture of how we would have the world.
Relate paint to
law,
to systems of thought,
to religions.

They are smoothings too.

At the store is a wall of paint colors, tabs to take home and
decide.
Ten blues,
Ten reds,
Twenty whites.
In dark greens alone there are
basil, billard green, hunt club, forestwood, bottle green, isle of
pines,
secret garden, rosemary, court yard,
and dozens of others.
How many light waves does one green vary from another?
Not many.
If I painted my office red,
say Incarnadine,
I would write differently.
If I painted my office black,
say onxy,
I would write differently.
But my office will be a kind of cream,
White Dove maybe.
So I will write what I write with that.

Blues skies; we are happy.
Stormy skies; we are tense.
Cloudy skies; we are ordinary.
And rainbows,
yes rainbows,
Roy G. Biv:
Red orange yellow green blue indigo violet.
I remember that from my high school science class,
about all I remember from my high school science class,

other than osmosis and something about a semi-permeable
membrane.
Rainbows make us happy.
Somewhere over the rainbow.
And double rainbows.
When I lived in Hawaii I learned about moonbows,
a circle of colors around a full moon.
I saw one in the dark of night.
Rariest of all, the double moonbow.
Most people who have lived in Hawaii all their lives have never
seen a double moonbow.
And the green flash.
On a boat out in the Pacific Ocean, sunrise,
time it perfectly to look at the horizon right when the sun appears,
and whap,
a green flash.
Most people haven't seen that either,
although one man I talked to claimed he just had.

I read once about a painter noted for his vivid colors who had a
car accident.
Not a huge crash, just a fender bender,
but he hit his head on the windshield.
From then on he could only see in black and white.
It, of course, changed his paintings entirely.
I wonder what the world would be like if we could only see in
black and white.
Stark,
basic,
or stylish like the 1920s.
Color gets in the way for a photographer,
gets in the way of the subject.
Distracts,

becomes a subject by itself.
A man in a black and white suit.
A man in a red suit.
A man in a purple plaid suit.
Not the same man, to someone seeing him.

So paint.
Artificial, sure, the way of the world.
I am glad we have colors,
and will stand by them.
They make the world more vivid,
even paint on dry wall.

And.

So much to write about.
And I only have so many years.
What percentage of everything will I cover?
2?
5?
11?
No not double figures.
I haven't even started writing about the stock market,
yogurt,
buzzards, all of them,
mufflers
hair dryers,
and the rest of the planet Earth.
Then there's the Milky Way.
The local galaxies.
The rest of the universe.
The others in the multiverse,
if that thought is correct.

I am so small that I am not even a quark.
Only my brain thinks in big terms,
infinity,
an infinity of infinities,
ten infinities times five infinities divided by two infinities.
And that really is a few cells in my head.
I reach out my hand,
and I am small again.

So which inch of the cosmic forever will I think about this
morning?
Clothes.
A man's fashion sense, i.e. my fashion sense:
dark pants, light shirt;
light pants, dark shirt.
I once knew, a bit, a very rich man;
he owned a skyscraper in Manhattan he had inherited from his
father.
Every time I saw him he wore the same: black pants and white
shirt.
Finally I asked him.
"I don't like deciding what to wear every day. I keep it simple,"
he said.
In his bedroom closet were two poles, top and bottom.
One held a row of white shirts; the other held a row of black
pants.
Simple.
T-shirts.
Right wing t-shirts, left wing t-shirts, t-shirts about dogs, t-shirts
about deer,
t-shirts about a song, t-shirts about presidential candidates, t-
shirts about car shows,
t-shirts about clubs, t-shirts about battles, t-shirts about TV shows

from the past.
I have one t-shirt with an Okra wearing boxing gloves.
I have another t-shirt with the words "Have a Crappie Day." Of course, it has a drawing of a fish.
Persona.
We express ourselves outwardly in many ways, many false, a few true, most just there.
My haircut. Am I really that short?
Grey flecks my brown hair now. Am I really brown flecked with gray?
One theory—I know I'm not a believer in theories—states that all poems and stories are
a projection of the writer's persona.
False.
A part.
Not the real person.
But then what is the real person?
The poem would be infinite.
A fourth of all my clothes are presents, from my wife, her family, my daughter.
Some, like that plaid pair of pants, I wouldn't have chosen for myself.
Others are the results of my Christmas list—by this time in life many of us give the others a list
of what we want.
My list is now 12 pages long.

I need a new suit.
All I have is a black, funeral one,
at least all I have that fit.
A red suit. Yah.
I see men wearing red suits at the Blues Music Awards in Memphis, so why not?

Purple. Not me, but I know somebody local who wears purple
suits.
Orange. University of Tennessee football fans wear orange suits.
Plaid?
Houndstooth. What a name. How about dripping fangs suits,
dark red.
A tuxedo.
Got one of those, but it has stayed in my closet for ten years
since my daughter's wedding.
All white. Mr. Clean, though I think he wears an undershirt.
Rainbow. A rainbow suit. Never seen one, but it's an interesting
idea.
Pin-striped. I'm a banker.
Just damn glad there's no photo of me wearing my '60s Nehru jacket.

I can't go to the grocery store nude, so I need clothes. My
persona, or at least part of it.
Camouflage and I might get into fights.

So clothes.
Haven't even scratched the surface of this subject,
one many people spend their lives on,
designers, manufacturers, sales.
But at least I brought it up.
Scratch.

Naruda's "Ode to My Socks" comes to mind.
Opens a new world.
"Ode to my underpants."
"Ode to my belt."
"'Ode to my kimono."

Think I will look up the Naruda poem and read it.
That's what I need right now.

And.

Three days to go before my arbitrary end to this poem.

And.

This will be short.
I didn't sleep much last night.
Amazing how our thoughts depend on sleep.
A really odd thing:
we lie horizontally, close our eyes, and a kind of darkness takes
over our brains.
With no outside senses, the brain uses what's in storage.
Then, say 8 hours later if we are lucky, we wake having had
adventures,
met old friends,
fought ghosts and demons,
and we are refreshed.
If we don't sleep deeply, our heads are pools.

My head is a pool.
Of dirty water.
Snakes slither.
Sharks.
Octopi.
Sea weed.
A sea pool.

So I don't want to write a lot today.
It would be all dithering.
More than usual.
A nap.
What a wonderful word.

And.

And.

Self-confidence.
It's really important.
Even diseases stay away from strong self-confidence.
Self-confidence means that a decade later
the person has a better job, a better marriage, a better everything.
He doesn't really strut.
She doesn't really stare.
They both do what they do,
and don't worry about those other people in the room.

Today I lack self-confidence.
Attacks on my job as professor—you don't work eight-hour
shifts; you sleep late; you think
only.
Attacks on my writing—it's your hobby because you don't make
money with your poems;
it doesn't do anything; nobody cares.
Attacks on me as a man—you're not Alpha; you haven't drilled
those holes in the cabinets;
you haven't painted the bedroom.
Attack, attack, attack.

Somehow, growing up in a problem family, I have a strong core
of self-confidence,
of pride.
I can have bad days when I feel low, below the belly of a toad.
I can give up,
for a while.
But somehow that core, like a hunk of stone, and yes it feels like

it's in my chest
and not my brain,
makes me look up, makes me smile at myself, makes me happy
at what I have done
in spite of continuous unending opposition.
Strutting, as I've written before, is not lording it over people who
think badly of you.
Strutting is keeping your eyes on the exit where you want to go,
of walking at a normal pace,
of smiling,
of not paying attention to those people.
Then out the exit
into the fresh air outside.
Those people don't count.
They are rednecks.
They only know their own lives.
You have so many possibilities.
Smile at the world.
Ignore the minds.
There are other minds elsewhere.

I am cool,
that's all I know.
You are cool.
That's all you know.

I am so self-confident
I am going to check my brain again for what is in storage there.
Argentina.
I would love to go to Argentina, the Indian north, the wine
country, Buenos Aires and the tango,
gaucho country as in *Don Segundo Sombra*, Ushaia.
The whole world is in quarantine now, so this is a wish list.

Not a bucket list.
I hate that idea.
I've got five things I want to do; O.K. I've done them; now I will
die.
The world is endless from our point of view.
So South Africa.
Three times I was supposed to teach in South Africa, but some-
thing happened,
Budget cutbacks mostly.
Nelson Mandela.
On my wall—I'm looking at it now—is a framed ballot from the
first free election in South Africa,
with Nelson Mandela's party, the ANC,
But also 19 other parties, like
Sports Organisation for Collective Contributions and Equal Rights
party,
and
the Keep It Straight and Simple party.
In America we generally can choose Democratic or Republican.
Maybe a few other useless parties, but basically two.
And Perth, Australia.
What an isolated city.
And Bora Bora.
And everywhere else.
I am in quarantine too; can't even visit some of the other states.
I want adventure, learning the new, meeting new people.
The old people are after my self-confidence.
The new would make my self-confidence bloom.

I hold my head up.
You hold your head up.
We are cool.

And.

And.

I was going to write until today,
then I saw that this will be the 28ᵗʰ day and file,
so I thought, maybe two more days.
Humans like round numbers, like 30.
They are easier for us to deal with.
100, 1 million, 10 trillion.
Much easier than say 8,642,951,
378,117,214,904,282,460,553,691,001,987,351,746,
even with the commas.
But
I am stopping this poem after this day, the 28ᵗʰ.
Neatness, roundness mean little to me.
Life is so messy.
The universe is so messy.
I don't think rounding off is God's way.
So The End.

But it's not really the end, as I've said before.
The End is not the end.
I will have thoughts after today,
probably write more poems,
stories,
emails,
Facebook postings.
Until death.

If I find that as a ghost I can still send email and post I will.
What is your address?

Bad night last night, little sleep, so I want to stop about here.
But can't.
I could rhyme, like a couplet, a culprit.
Life hurts and is full of misery so
laugh and love and make multitudes of dough.
No no no.
Can't stop there.

Dear reader.
We're in this together.
What are your thoughts?

And.

I was wrong.
I can't stop where I meant to yesterday.
This is the 29th day.
I want to say something else,
Though I'm not sure what it is.

Nothing ends.

That's it.
Nothing ends.

And to prove the point here is some more.
No big climax, no Rule of Three, no dead end street, no finish
line, no period.
That's what I will do.
No period

And